THE LITTLE BOOK OF

the nineteen **70s**

glitz, glam and liberation

OH!

CONTENTS

INTRODUCTION

As the world emerged from the turbulence of the 1970s, the 1970s set a new stage for global affairs. Cold War tensions persisted, but the decade also witnessed significant geopolitical shifts. The Vietnam War came to an end, the Watergate scandal shook the very foundations of American democracy, and the oil crisis of 1973 led to soaring inflation and rising energy costs.

As with the decade that preceded it, the 1970s was an era of intense protest and social activism. Civil rights movements continued to fight for equality, women's liberation and LGBTQ+ activism stepped up a gear, and environmentalism rose in response to growing ecological concerns. The world witnessed demonstrations, strikes and grassroots movements demanding change and challenging oppressive systems.

Of course, the 1970s also showcased a vibrant popular culture. Music genres like disco, rock, funk and punk flourished, while iconic films and books such as

The Godfather and *Slaughterhouse-Five* pushed the boundaries of storytelling. Fashion trends, ranging from the platform shoes and glittering outfits of disco to the torn jeans and leather jackets of punk, reflected the changing social landscape.

Innovations in the 1970s transformed the world, laying the foundation for the technological advancements that shape our lives today. The invention of the microprocessor revolutionized computing, giving birth to personal computers and setting the stage for the digital age. The development of ARPANET, the precursor to the internet, laid the groundwork for global connectivity, and breakthroughs in medicine, such as MRI scanning, ushered in a new era of healthcare.

This little book is a wonderful journey through the triumphs, challenges and ideas that defined the 1970s. Packed full of fabulous facts and quirky asides, as well as fascinating quotes from the era's movers and shakers, it's the perfect guide to this remarkable decade.

the nineteen 70s

revolutionary ripples

As the tumultuous 1960s drew to a close, the 1970s witnessed a remarkable shift in social, political and economic landscapes.

Amidst Cold War tensions, nations grappled with energy crises, the Watergate scandal shook the political world to its core, and the UK saw its first female prime minister. This chapter delves into the defining events, ideologies and aspirations that shaped the decade.

Student Massacre

On 4 May 1970, during a protest against the Vietnam War at Kent State University in Ohio, US, members of the Ohio National Guard fired at unarmed students. Four were killed and nine others were injured.

The incident sparked widespread outrage and protests across the nation, further fuelling opposition to the war.

66

I saw a body on the asphalt...
I walked to the dead person. I shot my
picture. Then I saw this young girl run
up – Mary Ann Vecchio. I knew I was
running out of film... Mary Ann knelt
next to a body. I didn't shoot right away
because it might have been my last
available frame. Mary Ann screamed.
I shot the picture, then two more.

99

John Filo

A journalism student whose iconic photograph of Jeffrey
Miller won him a Pulitzer Prize. The photo became the
lasting symbol of the tragedy.

Hard Times

The 1970s were marred by severe economic crises, with high inflation and stagnant economic growth affecting many nations.

The oil crisis of 1973 further exacerbated economic woes, leading to rising energy prices, unemployment and recessions.

"

We have an energy crisis, but there is no crisis of the American spirit.

"

Richard Nixon

Address given by the president, 7 November 1973

Just Watch Me

Pierre Trudeau, Canada's charismatic leader throughout the 1970s – and the father of future prime minister Justin Trudeau – championed bilingualism, multiculturalism and individual rights.

His memorable quote, "Just watch me" – a response when questioned on how far he would go in the suspension of civil liberties to maintain order – is still used in political discussion today.

Bloody Sunday

On 30 January 1972, during a civil
rights march in Derry, Northern Ireland,
British soldiers opened fire on unarmed
demonstrators. It resulted in the deaths of
13 people and went on to fuel tensions in
the region and significantly worsen
the conflict between nationalist and
unionist communities.

The event remains a painful chapter in the
history of the Troubles in Northern Ireland.

Scandal at the Top

The Watergate scandal, a watershed moment in American politics, began with a break-in at the Democratic National Committee headquarters at the Watergate complex in Washington, DC, in June 1972.

It was later revealed that the incident had been orchestrated by members of President Richard Nixon's administration, and evidence emerged of a massive cover-up, involving illegal wiretapping, bribes and obstruction of justice. Facing impeachment, Nixon resigned in 1974.

"

I am not a crook.

"

Richard Nixon

Talking to 400 Associated Press journalists in Walt Disney World, 16 November 1973. The phrase took on a life of its own and is listed at number one in *Time* magazine's "Top Ten Unfortunate Political One-Liners".

66

I have not sought this enormous responsibility, but I will not shirk it...

99

Gerald Ford

Remarks upon being sworn in as US president in the wake of Richard Nixon's resignation, 9 August 1974. Ford is the only person to become US president without winning an election for president or vice president.

66

I've never been one to say
that Britain was joining a
happy band of brothers.

99

James Callaghan
Prime minister of the UK from 1976 until 1979,
commenting on the UK's entry into the
Common Market in 1976

Munich Massacre

At the 1972 Summer Olympics, held in Munich, Germany, eight Palestinian terrorists killed two members of the Israeli Olympic team before taking nine more hostage.

Tragically, the situation escalated when a rescue attempt was mounted by German authorities. In the ensuing gunfire, all the hostages were killed, alongside a West German police officer and five of the terrorists.

"
They're all gone.
"

Jim McKay
ABC sportscaster who had been broadcasting from the
Olympic Village for 14 straight hours, delivering the worst
possible news on the fate of 11 Israeli hostages at the
Munich Olympics, 6 September 1972

Birth of Bangladesh

In 1971, a major conflict broke out between neighbouring India and Pakistan. It stemmed from the liberation movement in East Pakistan (now Bangladesh) and the subsequent military intervention by India in support of the independence movement.

The war resulted in the surrender of Pakistani forces, leading to the creation of Bangladesh as an independent nation.

66

The struggle this time is for emancipation, the struggle this time is for independence.

99

Sheikh Mujibur Rahman

The first president of Bangladesh, inspiring the Bengali nation to wage liberation war against the Pakistan occupation army, 7 March 1971. He was assassinated, alongside his family, on 15 August 1975

> **"**
> # I don't think there will be a woman prime minister in my time.
> **"**

Margaret Thatcher
in a BBC interview, 5 March 1973

“

The accumulation of nuclear arms has to be constrained if mankind is not to destroy itself.

”

Henry Kissinger
US Secretary of State, press conference held on
13 February 1974

❝

My fellow Americans, our long national nightmare is over. Our constitution works.

❞

Gerald Ford
Remarks upon being sworn in as US president,
9 August 1974

"

I've looked on a lot of women with lust. I've committed adultery in my heart many times.

"

Jimmy Carter

While running for president, in an interview with *Playboy Magazine*, 1976. The unfortunate remark was included in *Time* magazine's "Top 10 Unfortunate Political One-Liners".

War Ends

The Vietnam War, one of the most significant conflicts of the 20th century, ended in 1975 with the fall of Saigon and the reunification of Vietnam under communist rule. The war resulted in the loss of an estimated 1.3 million Vietnamese civilians and soldiers, as well as over 58,000 American military personnel.

The conflict also left devastating scars on the region, including the long-term impact of Agent Orange and other chemical weapons.

"

How do you ask a man to be the last man to die in Vietnam? How do you ask a man to be the last man to die for a mistake?

"

John Kerry

A Vietnam War veteran who later became a prominent US politician, in a speech to the US Congress, 22 April 1971

Cambodian Genocide

Carried out by the Khmer Rouge regime from 1975 to 1979, the genocide in Cambodia resulted in the deaths of an estimated 1.7 to 2.2 million people. Led by Pol Pot, the regime subjected the population to forced labour, executions and mass killings in an attempt to create an agrarian communist society.

The population was decimated, infrastructure was destroyed and survivors were traumatized for generations to come.

"

To keep you is no gain; to lose you is no loss.

"

Khmer Rouge mantra

Soweto Uprising

On 16 June 1976, thousands of black students in Soweto, South Africa, took to the streets to protest against the compulsory use of Afrikaans as the language of instruction in schools.

The protest quickly turned into a violent confrontation with the police, with many students shot and killed.

"

On June 17, I watched as bodies were dragged out of what had been a shopping centre on the Old Patch Road [sic]. I saw figures running out of the shop, some carrying goods.
They ran across the veld like wild animals, dropping like bags as bullets hit them... I thought the world had come to an end.

"

Nomavende Mathiane
Journalist, as quoted in Philip Bonner and Lauren Segal's
Soweto: A History, 1998

Jonestown Massacre

On 18 November 1978, more than 900 members of the Peoples Temple cult died after consuming cyanide-laced Kool-Aid.

Led by the cult's leader, Jim Jones, the mass murder-suicide event – which took place in the cult's remote settlement, Jonestown, in Guyana – remains the largest mass suicide in modern history.

"

If we can't live in peace, then let's die in peace.

"

Jim Jones
Leader of the Peoples Temple cult, on a
chilling audio tape discovered at the site of the
Jonestown massacre, November 1978

Revolution in Iran

The Iranian Revolution in 1979 led to the overthrow of Mohammad Reza Pahlavi – the shah of Iran – and the establishment of an Islamic republic under Ayatollah Khomeini.

It was marked by widespread protests, strikes and political unrest, culminating in the shah's departure from Iran.

"

I shall never forget the tears in the eyes of the shah the day we left Iran. In that deserted runway and in the aircraft, my only thought was whether it was the last time or would [we ever] return.

"

Farah Pahlavi

Widow of Mohammad Reza Pahlav, the last shah of Iran, recalling the Iranian Revolution, 27 July 2010

Hostage Crisis

At the close of the decade, on 4 November 1979, a group of Iranian students, supporters of the Iranian Revolution, stormed the US Embassy in Tehran. Taking 52 Americans hostage, they held them captive for 444 days until their release on 20 January 1981.

The crisis started as a response to the US granting asylum to the recently deposed shah of Iran, Mohammad Reza Pahlavi, which further strained relations between the two countries.

"

I wish I had sent one more helicopter to get the hostages, and we would've rescued them, and I would've been re-elected.

"

Jimmy Carter
Former US president, reflecting on how the Iranian hostage crisis ruined his chances of re-election

Iron Lady

On 4 May 1979, Margaret Thatcher became the UK's first female prime minister. She would bring about a significant shift in British politics, introducing conservative economic policies, reducing the power of trade unions and advocating for free-market principles.

Dubbed the "Iron Lady" for her uncompromising leadership style, her policies would have a profound impact on the political landscape of the era.

66

Any woman who understands
the problems of running
a home will be nearer to
understanding the problems
of running a country.

99

Margaret Thatcher
In the year she became prime minister, 1979

Serial Killer

In June 1975, notorious American serial killer Ted Bundy was put on trial in Florida for the murders of two young women, Kimberly Leach and Margaret Bowman. It was the first trial to be televized nationally.

Handsome, educated and charming, Bundy did not fit the serial killer mould. He later confessed to killing at least 30 women across 30 states between 1974 and 1978, though the actual number of his victims remains unknown. He was executed in 1989.

❝

I don't think anybody doubts whether I've done some bad things. The question is: what, of course, and how and, maybe even most importantly, why?

❞

Ted Bundy

The notorious murderer in an interview with Bob Keppel days before his execution, January 1989

New Pope

In October 1978, the Catholic Church welcomed a new pope. John Paul II, born Karol Józef Wojtyła, was the first non-Italian pope in over 450 years. Known for his charismatic leadership, extensive travels and conservative stance on social and theological issues, he played a crucial role in advocating for human rights and promoting interfaith dialogue. He served as pope until his death in 2005.

"

Do not be afraid. Do not be satisfied with mediocrity. Put out into the deep and let down your nets for a catch.

"

John Paul II
Inaugural homily, St Peter's Square,
Vatican City, 22 October 1978

"

Where there is discord,
may we bring harmony.
Where there is error, may we
bring truth. Where there is
doubt, may we bring faith.
And where there is despair,
may we bring hope.

"

Margaret Thatcher
Quoting St Francis of Assisi, on her election victory,
4 May 1979

❝

Love begins at home, and
it is not how much we do, but
how much love we put in the
action that we do.

❞

Mother Teresa
From her acceptance speech for the Nobel Peace Prize,
11 December 1979

the nineteen 70s

Chapter 2

activism and awakening

The 1970s was an era when civil rights movements, women's liberation, environmentalism and anti-war protests continued to gain momentum.

As activists took to the streets to challenge oppressive systems, their efforts led to landmark achievements in civil rights legislation, the advancement of gender and LGBTQ+ equality and heightened environmental awareness.

Earth Day

The first Earth Day took place on 22 April 1970. Across the US, an estimated 20 million people attended events to raise awareness of environmental issues.

Earth Day is now observed in 192 countries.

“

Man must stop pollution and conserve his resources, not merely to enhance existence but to save the race from intolerable deterioration and possible extinction.

”

New York Times editorial, the day after the first Earth Day, 23 April 1970

Ms. Magazine

In 1972, prominent US feminists Gloria Steinem and Dorothy Pitman Hughes founded this outspoken and hard-hitting publication to discuss women's issues, politics and culture. It is still running today.

"

Ms. was a brazen act of independence in the 1970s... Most magazines marketed to women were limited to advice about finding a husband, saving marriages, raising babies or using the right cosmetics.

"

From the *Ms.* magazine website

Black Pride

Following the gains of the 1960s civil rights movement, the 1970s saw a flourishing of black art, literature and cultural expression. Figures such as poet and playwright Amiri Baraka (formerly LeRoi Jones), musicians Nina Simone and Marvin Gaye, and visual artist Faith Ringgold used their art to address social and political issues faced by black communities.

"

I was always a politician from the day the civil rights people chose me as their protest singer.

"

Nina Simone

Women's Liberation

The Women's Strike for Peace and Equality took place in New York City on 26 August 1970.

Thousands of women participated in the day-long strike and demonstrations, demanding gender equality and an end to discrimination in all aspects of life. This historic event helped to galvanize the feminist movement of the 1970s.

"

Don't iron while the strike is hot.

"

Feminist slogan from the Women's Strike for Peace
and Equality, New York City, 26 August 1970

Gay Liberation Day

Stemming from the Stonewall Riots of the previous year, this historic gathering, held on 28 June 1970 in New York City, marked the first anniversary of the LGBTQ+ community's fight for equality and rights.

Thousands took to the streets, proudly proclaiming their identities and demanding societal change. The spirit of resilience and activism that emerged laid the foundation for the modern LGBTQ+ rights movement worldwide.

" Say it loud, gay is proud. "

Chant at the Gay Liberation Day march,
New York City, 28 June 1970

"

It is not our differences that divide us. It is our inability to recognize, accept and celebrate those differences.

"

Audre Lorde
The celebrated activist and author who described herself as a "black, lesbian, feminist, mother, poet, warrior"

"

Any woman who chooses to
behave like a full human being
should be warned that the
armies of the status quo will treat
her as something of a dirty joke...
She will need her sisterhood.

"

Gloria Steinhem
New York Magazine, 20 December 1971

" What will you do? "

Germain Greer

The famous last line of Greer's groundbreaking feminist work, *The Female Eunuch*, which called upon women to question everything they had been taught about sex, love, their bodies and their rights, 1970

Aboriginal Land Rights

After many years of struggle, the passing of the Aboriginal Land Rights (Northern Territory) Act in Australia granted Indigenous people a legal mechanism to regain control over some of their ancestral lands.

It was the first attempt by an Australian government to legally recognize the Aboriginal system of land ownership, and marked a significant step toward addressing historical injustices.

American Indian Movement

Drawing inspiration from the 1960s civil rights movement, Native Americans grew increasingly vocal in their demands for equal rights.

Staging demonstrations and occupations, they called for recognition of sovereignty, protested broken treaties and advocated for self-determination.

66

If we are not our brother's keeper, at least let us not be his executioner.

99

Marlon Brando
Declining his Best Actor Oscar (for *The Godfather*)
in support of Native Americans, published in the
New York Times, 30 March 1973

Gay Rights Champion

In November 1978, Harvey Milk, a pioneering gay rights activist and the first openly gay elected official in California, was shot and killed by a former colleague.

Milk's assassination sent shockwaves through the LGBTQ+ community and beyond, galvanizing the fight for equal rights. His legacy as a champion for gay rights and social justice continues to inspire and shape LGBTQ+ activism.

"

If a bullet should enter my brain, let that bullet destroy every closet door in the country.

"

Harvey Milk

From a tape to be played in the event of his assasination

the nineteen 70s

groove and glam

The music scene in the 1970s exploded with genres such as disco, rock, funk and punk. Disco's vibrant beats dominated dance floors, while rock artists pushed boundaries with experimental sounds.

Meanwhile, fashion embraced a fusion of styles, from the disco glam of sequinned outfits and platform shoes to the rebellious punk aesthetic of ripped jeans and leather jackets.

"

There are parts I can't remember.

"

Elton John

Reflecting on the 1970s, as quoted in Tom Doyle's
*Captain Fantastic: Elton John's Stellar Trip through the
'70s*, 2017

❝

I think Led Zeppelin must have worn some of the most peculiar clothing that men had ever been seen to wear without cracking a smile.

❞

Robert Plant
Lead singer, Led Zeppelin

Rock Icons

In 1970, the music world was rocked by the tragic deaths of two legendary artists. Guitarist Jimi Hendrix, who was known for his electrifying performances, passed away on 18 September, and the enigmatic singer Janis Joplin died on 4 October.

The stars' untimely deaths, both at the age of 27, left a profound void in the music industry.

"

On stage, I make love to 25,000 different people, then I go home alone.

"

Janis Joplin

Let it Be

The Beatles – one of the world's most iconic bands – officially called it quits in 1970. Their final album, *Let It Be*, was released on 8 May, one month after Paul McCartney announced the group's breakup.

The making of the legendary album was marked by a period of diverging creative paths, business disagreements and frequent walk-outs.

66

I am not the person who instigated the split. Oh no, no, no. John walked into a room one day and said 'I am leaving the Beatles'. Is that instigating the split, or not?

99

Paul McCartney

Setting the record straight on the 1970 Beatles split, in an interview aired on 23 October 2021

"

When I was about 12, I used to think I must be a genius, but nobody's noticed. If there is such a thing as a genius, I am one, and if there isn't, I don't care.

"

John Lennon
Rolling Stone, 1970

66

I think in the '70s that there was a general feeling of chaos, a feeling that the idea of the '60s as 'ideal' was a misnomer. Nothing seemed ideal anymore. Everything seemed in-between.

99

David Bowie

" Frankly, it is very hard to remember things from the 1970s. "

Glen Campbell

66

I wrote 'Big Yellow Taxi' on my first trip to Hawaii. I took a taxi to the hotel and when I woke up the next morning, I threw back the curtains and saw these beautiful green mountains in the distance. Then, I looked down and there was a parking lot as far as the eye could see, and it broke my heart this blight on paradise. That's when I sat down and wrote the song.

99

Joni Mitchell

Reflecting on her iconic song "Big Yellow Taxi", which was released in 1970

Waterloo

Released in 1974, ABBA's "Waterloo" won the Eurovision Song Contest and catapulted them to international stardom. With its catchy melodies, vibrant harmonies and infectious energy, the track showcased ABBA's unique sound and set the stage for their global success.

It became an anthem for the band, laying the foundation for their subsequent chart-topping hits throughout the 1970s and beyond.

"

In my honest opinion, we looked like NUTS in those years.

"

Björn Ulvaues
Member of ABBA, reflecting on the 1970s

Groovy Trends

From flares and bell sleeves to miniskirts and platform shoes, the 1970s witnessed an eclectic mix of style influences. The rise of disco introduced shimmering fabrics and bell-bottom trousers, while the bohemian look embraced flowing maxi dresses and fringe details.

Glam rock brought flamboyant outfits and glittering accessories, and punk fashion emerged with ripped jeans, band t-shirts and leather jackets.

66

Every model's dream [is] to be on the cover of *Vogue*. You have arrived when you made the cover of *Vogue*. And then when I found out I was the first person of colour on the cover and what that meant, I was like, wow, this is really a big deal.

99

Beverly Johnson

The model made history when she became the first African-American to appear on the cover of *Vogue* magazine in the US, in August 1974

Fashion Rebel

Punk icon Vivienne Westwood opened her first boutique, Let It Rock, on London's Kings Road in 1971. A year later, the shop was renamed Too Fast To Live, Too Young To Die, and by 1974, it had become Sex, with the provocative slogan "Rubberwear for the office."

The name changed again to Seditionaries before finally becoming Worlds End in 1980 – the name it has to this day.

66

Fashion is very important.
It is life-enhancing and, like
everything that gives pleasure, it
is worth doing well.

99

Vivienne Westwood
The fashion designer who viewed punk as "seeing if
one could put a spoke in the system"

Five Fashion Icons

From the whimsical style of Fleetwood Mac's Stevie Nicks to the edgy cool of Debbie Harry, the 1970s saw a wide array of fashion trends.

Bianca Jagger – the wife of Rolling Stone Mick Jagger, Bianca was a fan of tube tops, chokers, sequins and berets.

Diana Ross – the very definition of disco glamour, Ross modelled silk bias-cut gowns, platform heels, sparkling mini-dresses and oversized fur coats.

Debbie Harry – the godmother of the New York punk scene, Blondie's lead singer strutted her stuff in mini-dresses, leather jackets and over-the-knee latex boots.

Ali Macgraw – This raven-haired American actress was all about bohemian blouses, mini dresses and tall leather boots.

Stevie Nicks – the Fleetwood Mac star sported fringed waistcoats, flared sleeves, capes and suede boots.

"

That feeling of gaining my independence and wanting it for every woman is what gave me the drive.

"

Diane von Furstenberg

Designer who rose to fame in the 1970s, September 1977

"

I've always liked long, flowing clothes... I used to rummage around in my grandmother's trunks trying to find them.

"

Stevie Nicks
Member of Fleetwood Mac and 1970s style icon

Grammy First

In 1974, Stevie Wonder achieved a remarkable feat at the Grammy Awards when his album *Innervisions* won Album of the Year. He was the first black artist to receive the honour. Additionally, the album's single "Superstition" won Best Male Pop Vocal Performance.

This recognition not only highlighted Stevie Wonder's immense talent but broke down barriers for future artists.

66

I never thought of being
blind as a disadvantage,
and I never thought of being
black as a disadvantage.

99

Stevie Wonder

Ten Iconic Tunes

"Bohemian Rhapsody"
Queen

"Stairway to Heaven"
Led Zeppelin

"Born to Run"
Bruce Springsteen

"Hotel California"
Eagles

"Heroes"
David Bowie

"Imagine"
John Lennon

"Your Song"
Elton John

"You're the One That I Want"
John Travolta and Olivia Newton-John

"Bridge Over Troubled Water"
Simon and Garfunkel

"Go Your Own Way"
Fleetwood Mac

It's going to be number one for centuries.

"

Kenny Everett
BBC radio DJ, after hearing Queen's "Bohemian Rhapsody"
for the first time, 1975

"

Punk rock isn't something you grow out of. Punk rock is an attitude, and the essence of that attitude is 'give us some truth'.

"

Joe Strummer
Lead singer of The Clash

Disco Fever

By the mid-1970s, disco music dominated the airwaves and dance floors. With its infectious beats, pulsating rhythms and catchy melodies, it became synonymous with vibrant nightlife and carefree dancing.

Iconic disco hits like "Stayin' Alive" by the Bee Gees and the success of movies like *Saturday Night Fever* propelled disco into the mainstream. The disco movement created a cultural phenomenon, influencing fashion, dance styles and the popular culture of the era.

5 Disco Hits

"Dancing Queen"
Abba (1976)

"Stayin' Alive"
Bee Gees (1977)

"Le Freak"
by Chic (1978)

"I Will Survive"
Gloria Gaynor (1978)

"YMCA"
Village People (1978)

Punk Rock

The birth of punk rock in the 1970s marked a rebellious and raw movement in music. Emerging in both the United States and the United Kingdom, bands like the Ramones, Sex Pistols and The Clash challenged mainstream conventions with their fast, aggressive sound and confrontational lyrics.

Punk rock became a symbol of youth rebellion and anti-establishment sentiments, and made a lasting impact on the music scene.

"

Hey! Ho! Let's go!

"

The Ramones

From the American punk rock band's hit "Blitzkrieg Bop"

The King is Dead

The iconic "King of Rock and Roll", Elvis Presley, passed away at his Graceland home on 16 August 1977. His sudden death at the age of 42 shocked the world.

Elvis' impact on popular culture was unparalleled, with his distinctive voice, charismatic performances and unique style revolutionizing the music scene.

"

The first time that I appeared on stage, it scared me to death. I really didn't know what all the yelling was about. I didn't realize that my body was moving. It's a natural thing to me. So to the manager backstage I said, 'What'd I do? What'd I do?' And he said, 'Whatever it is, go back and do it again.'

"

Elvis Presley

From a taped interview used in MGM's documentary
Elvis on Tour, 1972

Mainstream Rap

In 1979, The Sugarhill Gang released "Rapper's Delight".

The first rap song to be played on the radio, it became a popular hit.

"

I said-a hip, hop, the hippie,
the hippie

To the hip hip hop-a you
don't stop the rock...

"

From "Rapper's Delight" by the Sugarhill Gang, 1979

the nineteen 70s

Chapter 4

artistic waves

The decade witnessed a flourishing of artistic expression and literary exploration that reflected the cultural and social shifts of the era.

Performance art, minimalism and pop art challenged traditional art forms while literature pushed boundaries and broke taboos, exploring themes of sex, race, identity and counterculture.

Minimalism

This prominent art movement was characterized by its simplicity and reduction of visual elements.

Artists embraced geometric forms, clean lines and monochromatic palettes, aiming to create works devoid of emotional expression or narrative content.

66

It is what it is, and it ain't nothin'
else... Everything is clearly,
openly, plainly delivered.

99

Dan Flavin
Prominent Minimalist artist

The Dinner Party

This installation artwork, created by Judy Chicago, features a triangular table with 39 place settings representing historical and mythical women.

Celebrating women's contributions to society, "The Dinner Party" sparked discussions about gender and the role of women in history and the modern world.

"

I am trying to make art that relates to the deepest and most mythic concerns of human kind and I believe that, at this moment of history, feminism is humanism.

"

Judy Chicago
Prominent feminist artist in the 1970s

Pushing Boundaries

Artists such as Marina Abramović, Chris Burden and Yoko Ono used their bodies as a medium to explore themes of identity, politics and social norms.

Performances often involved endurance, physical risk and audience participation, blurring the lines between art and life and provoking visceral reactions.

66

Art is my life and my life is art.

99

Yoko Ono

Leading performance artist in the 1970s

Celebrity Art

Andy Warhol continued to explore his signature style of Pop Art in the 1970s. His endeavours included collaborations with various celebrities, such as Mick Jagger, Muhammad Ali and Pelé.

Warhol took dozens of commissions a year, charging about $25,000 (£19,500) per painting.

"

I said that athletes were
better than movie stars and
I don't know what I'm talking
about because athletes are
the new movie stars.

"

Andy Warhol
Writing in his diary after being commissioned to create
a series of athlete portraits, 1977

Performance Art

In 1975, Marina Abramović's notorious "Lips of Thomas" broke new ground. Lying atop blocks of ice, she cut and flagellated herself, pushing her body to its physical limits while gesturing toward the abuse that female bodies have endured throughout history.

The Sydney Opera House

This architectural masterpiece opened in October 1973.

Designed by Danish architect Jørn Utzon, the building project was plagued by delays, engineering challenges and a massive budget overspend. Despite this, the opera house, with its distinctive shell-shaped sails, is now considered one of the world's most iconic buildings.

"

Finally, a book that talks frankly about sex without being prim or prurient, and about religion without scolding or condescending.

"

Lev Grossman
Writing in *Time* magazine about Judy Blume's taboo-breaking novel for pre-teens, *Are You There God? It's Me, Margaret*, 1970

"

A custom-crafted study of paranoia, a spew from the 1960s and – in all its hysteria, insolence, insult and rot – a desperate and important book, a wired nightmare, the funniest piece of American prose.

"

Crawford Woods

Reviewing Hunter S. Thompson's novel,
Fear and Loathing in Las Vegas, 23 July 1972

66

Gravity's Rainbow is bone-crushingly dense, compulsively elaborate, silly, obscene, funny, tragic, pastoral, historical, philosophical, poetic, grindingly dull, inspired, horrific, cold, bloated, beached and blasted.

99

Richard Locke

Review of Thomas Pynchon's challenging masterpiece, *Gravity's Rainbow*, 11 March 1973

66

And for a future, I didn't want a split-level home with a station wagon, pastel refrigerator and a houseful of blonde children evenly spaced through the years. I didn't want to walk into the pages of *McCall's* magazine and become the model housewife. I didn't even want a husband or any man for that matter. I wanted to go my own way.

99

Rita Mae Brown

Rubyfruit Jungle, 1973. The novel caused a stir for its groundbreaking and explicit portrayal of lesbianism.

5 Literary Gems

The Bluest Eye
Toni Morrison (1970)

This pioneering novel, with a young black girl at its heart, established the voice of one of America's greatest novelists.

Fear of Flying
Erica Jong (1973)

Exploring female sexuality, identity and the quest for freedom, this candid and provocative novel changed the way the western world talked about sex.

Gravity's Rainbow
Thomas Pynchon (1973)

This hugely controversial novel covers war, sex, drugs, chemistry, history and psychology – amongst other things.

Zen and the Art of MotorCycle Maintenance
Robert Persig (1974)

This philosophical work about a road trip across the western US was rejected 126 times before it was accepted for publication.

The Shining
Stephen King (1977)

King's disturbing novel, delving into the terrifying isolation of the Overlook Hotel and one man's descent into madness, has become one of the most enduring horror stories ever written.

Hitchhiker's Guide to the Galaxy

Published in 1979, Douglas Adams' sci-fi romp across the universe explores the legitimacy of authority, the absurdity of bureaucracy and the very meaning of life.

A number one bestseller, it is arguably one of the most famous science fiction books ever written.

"

He was wrong to think
he could now forget that the
big, hard, oily, dirty, rainbow-
hung Earth on which he lived
was a microscopic dot on a
microscopic dot lost in the
unimaginable infinity of
the Universe.

"

Douglas Adams

Hitchhiker's Guide to the Galaxy, 1979

"

It's the work that brought down a presidency and launched a thousand reporting careers.

"

Alex Altman

Reviewing Carl Bernstein and Bob Woodward,
All the President's Men (1974), *Time* magazine,
17 August 2011

"

[It] should in no way be associated with that great body of factual information relating to orthodox Zen Buddhist practice. It's not very factual on motorcycles, either.

"

Robert Persig

Introduction to Persig's book, *Zen and the Art of Motorcycle Maintenance*, 1974

the nineteen 70s

thrills and triumphs

Sporting events, such as the legendary "Thrilla in Manila" between boxers Muhammad Ali and Joe Frazier, wowed audiences, while the rise of iconic athletes like Billie Jean King captivated the world.

In entertainment, films such as *Star Wars* and *The Godfather* became instant classics, and the Atari 2600 video game console brought arcade-style gaming into the home.

"

They always say time changes
things, but you actually have to
change them yourself.

"

Andy Warhol
The Philosophy of Andy Warhol, 1975

66

I slept with some nerd. I hope it was George [Lucas]... I took too many drugs to remember.

99

Carrie Fisher
Reflecting on how she got cast in *Star Wars*

66

My goal is to win the
World Chess Championship;
to beat the Russians. I take
this very seriously.

99

Bobby Fischer

Fischer beat Russian Boris Spassky to become the World
Chess Champion on 31 August 1972. The victory ended a
Soviet win streak that dated back to 1948.

"

I'm taking this match
very seriously. I love to win.
I welcome the responsibility
and the pressure. Bobby had
better be ready.

"

Billie Jean King

Ahead of her 1973 match against former number one
tennis player Bobby Riggs, who put out a claim that no
woman could beat him. The match, won by Billie Jean King
in straight sets, was dubbed "The Battle of the Sexes", and
drew a worldwide TV audience of 90 million.

"The Greatest"

Muhammad Ali dominated the 1970s with his boxing prowess and charisma.

His iconic matches against Joe Frazier and George Foreman made him the undisputed heavyweight champion, while his refusal to be drafted into the Vietnam War solidified his status as a symbol of protest and social change.

"

I am America. I am the part you won't recognize. But get used to me. Black, confident, cocky; my name, not yours; my religion, not yours; my goals, my own; get used to me.

"

Muhammad Ali
1970

Catchphrases

From classic sitcoms to thrilling dramas, the following memorable lines have become part of TV culture history:

"Who loves ya, baby?"
Kojak (1973–78)

"Dy-no-mite!"
Good Times (1974–79)

"Up your nose with a rubber hose!"
Welcome Back, Kotter (1975–79)

"Good night, John-Boy"
The Waltons (1972–81)

"Just one more thing..."
Columbo (1971–78)

"God'll get you for that"
Maude (1972–78)

"Sit on it!"
Happy Days (1974–84)

"Whatcha talkin' 'bout, Willis?"
Diff'rent Strokes (1978–86)

66
He's not the Messiah, he's a very naughty boy.
99

Terry Jones
Monty Python's Life of Brian, 1979

❝

A relationship, I think, is like a shark. You know? It has to constantly move forward or it dies. And I think what we got on our hands is a dead shark.

❞

Alvy Singer

As played by Woody Allen, in *Annie Hall*, 1977

Bruce Lee

The martial artist and actor became a global icon in the 1970s, starring in martial arts films such as *Enter the Dragon* and *Fists of Fury*.

His philosophy of Jeet Kune Do and his dedication to physical and mental discipline inspired countless martial artists, leaving behind a powerful legacy even after his untimely death in 1973.

66

Empty your mind.
Be formless, shapeless, like
water... Be water, my friend.

99

Bruce Lee
Playing the character Li Tsung, a martial arts instructor,
in an episode of *Longstreet*, 1971

"

It's not personal, Sonny. It's strictly business.

"

Michael Corelone

As played by Al Pacino, *The Godfather*, 1972

"

Loneliness has followed me my
whole life; everywhere.
In bars, in cars, sidewalks, stores,
everywhere. There's no escape.

"

Travis Bickle
As played by Robert de Niro, *Taxi Driver*, 1976

"You're gonna need a bigger boat.

Martin Brody
Playing the police chief in the film *Jaws*, 1975

"

I love the smell of napalm in the morning!

"

Lieutenant Colonel Kilgore
Played by Robert Duvall, to his fellow soldiers,
Apocalypse Now, 1979

Five Fabulous Films

The Godfather

dir. Francis Ford Coppola (1972)

Now considered a cinematic masterpiece, this exploration of organized crime features iconic performances and powerful storytelling.

The Exorcist

dir. William Friedkin (1973)

A groundbreaking horror film that shocked audiences worldwide with its terrifying depiction of demonic possession.

Jaws
dir. Steven Spielberg (1975)

This summer blockbuster about a predatory shark instilled fear of the ocean with its thrilling suspense and iconic theme music.

Taxi Driver
dir. Martin Scorsese (1976)

This gritty and introspective portrayal of urban alienation features a compelling performance from Robert de Niro in the lead role.

Annie Hall
dir. Woody Allen (1977)

Showcasing Allen's trademark wit and self-depreciating humour, this romantic comedy won multiple Academy Awards, including Best Picture.

Star Wars

In 1977, this film directed by George Lucas, ignited a global phenomenon. Featuring epic storytelling, groundbreaking special effects and memorable characters, it captivated audiences.

The film's imaginative universe, iconic music and the timeless battle between good and evil have become a cornerstone of science fiction storytelling.

"

May the force be with you.

"

This iconic line from *Star Wars* is first said by
General Jan Dodonna just before the Rebel pilots are about
to launch into the Battle of Yavin

Top Toys

From classic favourites like Barbie and Hot Wheels to the rise of electronic gaming with Atari, the era offered a range of toys that fuelled imagination and creativity.

Rubik's Cube – Invented by Hungarian-born Ernő Rubik in 1974, this three-dimensional puzzle became a worldwide sensation.

Atari 2600 – The home video game console brought arcade-style gaming into the home, with titles like Pong and Space Invaders captivating players.

Spirograph – First launched in the UK in 1965, this geometric drawing toy, consisting of interlocking plastic gears and pens, became a firm favourite.

Stretch Armstrong – This stretchable action figure, filled with gel-like material, allowed kids to pull and twist him in all directions.

Big Wheel – Featuring a low-slung seat and a large front wheel for easy riding and thrilling spins, this tricycle became a favourite among kids.

Super Simon – This handheld electronic memory game challenged players to remember and repeat a sequence of lights and sounds.

Space Invaders

Pong, released by Atari in 1972, was a simple yet addictive video game that simulated table tennis.

Space Invaders, launched in 1978, introduced players to the thrill of shooting down descending alien invaders. A landmark title in the history of video games, it paved the way for its future growth and innovation.

66
Don't watch TV tonight. Play it!
99

Atari advertisement promoting its groundbreaking video computer system that allowed users to play video games on their TV sets, 1979

Pet Rock

One of the strangest fads of the 1970s was the craze for the Pet Rock toy. Created by entrepreneur Gary Dahl, the "pet" was literally a plain rock in a box accompanied by a care manual – which featured tips on everything from feeding to obedience training, and even provided a lineage, such as the Egyptian Pyramids. The rocks flew off the shelves and made their creator a millionaire.

"

'Come' – it is essential that your PET ROCK learns this command. A rock that doesn't come when it's called will cause its owner endless embarrassment.

"

From the manual for the Pet Rock, one of the biggest selling toys in the mid-70s

Walt Disney World

Opening on 1 October 1971, in Bay Lake,
Florida, the park featured rides
and attractions such as Cinderella Castle,
Jungle Cruise, The Haunted Mansion
and Snow White's Scary Adventures.

66

May Walt Disney World bring joy and inspiration and new knowledge to all who come to this happy place... a magic kingdom where the young at heart of all ages can laugh and play and learn together.

99

Roy O. Disney

Dedication read by one of the Disney brothers at the official opening of Disney World in Orlando, Florida, US, 1 October 1971

M*A*S*H

Launched in 1972, this critically acclaimed comedy-drama series was set during the Korean War. Powerfully blending humour and wit with poignant storytelling, the show explored the camaraderie and challenges of the Mobile Army Surgical Hospital unit.

Packed full of memorable characters, M*A*S*H has left a lasting legacy as one of television's most influential and beloved shows.

"

War isn't hell. War is war,
and hell is hell. And of the two,
war is a lot worse.

"

Hawkeye Pierce
As played by Alan Alda, *M*A*S*H*, Season 5:
"The General's Practitioner"

Streaking Craze

Streaking became an outrageous cultural phenomenon in the 1970s. Shedding their inhibitions, streakers darted across stadiums, university campuses and public spaces, baring it all in a wild display of exhibitionism.

It blurred the lines between scandalous and hilarious, blending shock, amusement and defiance.

"

Isn't it fascinating to think
that probably the only laugh
that man will ever get in his life
is by stripping off and showing
his shortcomings?

"

David Niven

Commenting on the man who streaked past him as he was
about to introduce Elizabeth Taylor at the 1974 Oscars

Thrilla in Manila

This monumental boxing match – now considered one of the most thrilling matches of all time – between Muhammad Ali and Joe Frazier took place in October 1975, in Manila, Philippines.

Lasting for 14 gruelling rounds, it was the third and final bout in the pair's fierce rivalry, with Ali emerging the victor. The fight showcased the champion's resilience and determination, and cemented his title as "the greatest of all time".

66

The main turning point of the fight came very late... when one of two tremendous right-hand smashes sent the gum shield sailing out of Frazier's mouth. The sight of this man actually moving backwards seemed to inspire Ali. I swear he hit Frazier with 30 tremendous punches... during the 14th round. He was dredging up all his own last reserves of power to make sure there wouldn't have to be a fifteenth round.

99

Frank McGhee
Daily Mirror, 2 October 1975

Historic First

American tennis player Arthur Ashe achieved an iconic victory at Wimbledon in 1975. In a thrilling final, he defeated the defending champion, Jimmy Connors, in four sets.

Ashe was the first and, to date, only black man to win the singles title at Wimbledon.

"

Start Where You Are. Use What You Have. Do What You Can.

"

Arthur Ashe

The first black man to win the Wimbledon tennis championship, in 1975

Charlie's Angels

In September 1976, this crime drama debuted on American TV and ran for five seasons, until 1981. The show followed the adventures of three female private detectives.

Mixing action, humour and iconic '70s fashion, *Charlie's Angels* was hugely popular with TV audiences – despite the accusation from some critics that it was shallow, escapist "Jiggle TV".

66

When the show was number
three, I figured it was our acting.
When it got to be number one,
I decided it could only be
because none of us wears a bra.

99

Farrah Fawcett
The actress, who played Jill Munroe in *Charlie's Angels*,
comments on the show's success, 1976

the nineteen 70s

Chapter 6

decade of discovery

The 1970s witnessed remarkable innovations across various fields.

From the development of ARPANET, the precursor to the internet, and the launch of one of the first personal computers, the Apple II, to medical breakthroughs in the form of MRI scanning and the world's first test tube baby, the decade's breakthroughs continue to influence our lives today.

Dawn of the Jumbo Age

On 22 January 1970, the world's first jumbo jet – a Boeing 747-100 – completed its first commercial flight.

Flying from New York to London, the aircraft carried 332 passengers and 18 crew members.

VCR

The first commercially successful videocassette recorder (VCR) appeared in 1971.

The introduction of more affordable VCR formats, such as VHS (Video Home System) by JVC, and Betamax by Sony, made it easier for people to capture personal moments, create their own home movies and record and play back TV shows at home.

"

Imagination will often carry us to worlds that never were, but without it we go nowhere.

"

Carl Sagan

Astronomer and one of the most famous scientists in the US in the 1970s

""

The dangers that face the world can, every one of them, be traced back to science. The salvations that may save the world will, every one of them, be traced back to science.

""

Isaac Asimov

Widely considered to be one of the best sci-fi writers of all time, Asimov penned these words in his collection of non-fiction science essays, *Today and Tomorrow and...*, 1973

Space Race

The Space Race between the US and the Soviet Union continued in the 1970s, but the focus shifted from manned lunar missions to space exploration and research.

Significant events included the US Apollo missions and the Soviet launch of the world's first space station, Salyut.

"
Okay, Houston... we've had a problem here.
,,

Jack Swigert

The phrase uttered by Swigert, the command module pilot of Apollo 13, after an explosion occurred on board the spacecraft on its way to the moon, 14 April 1970. For the 1995 film, *Apollo 13*, the phrase was altered to "Houston, we have a problem".

Pocket Calculator

Sinclair pocket calculators revolutionized the industry and brought advanced technology to the masses.

Introduced in 1972, the Sinclair Executive featured a sleek design and a bright red LED display and was known for its low cost and compact size.

"

There is no reason why anyone would want a computer in their home.

"

Ken Olsen

Founder of the Digital Equipment Corporation, 1977

World Trade Center

New York's iconic Twin Towers – standing 415 metres feet high and at the time the tallest buildings in the world – were officially opened in April 1973. Each of the towers had 110 floors, and on windy days, could sway up to 30 cm side to side.

In 1973, the Sears Tower – now known as the Willis Tower – opened in Chicago, overtaking the World Trade Center as the tallest building in the world.

66

The World Trade Center is a living symbol
of man's dedication to world peace...
beyond the compelling need to make
this a monument to world peace, the
World Trade Center should, because of
its importance, become a representation
of man's belief in humanity, his need
for individual dignity, his belief in the
cooperation of men, and through this
cooperation, his ability to find greatness.

99

Minoru Yamasaki
Chief architect of the World Trade Center Complex, remarks
at the opening ceremonies and dedication, 4 April 1973

Lucy

In 1974, anthropologists made an incredible discovery in Ethiopia.

Led by Donald Johanson, the scientists uncovered the fossilized remains of a female hominid belonging to the species *Australopithecus afarensis*.

The hominid – given the name "Lucy" – lived approximately 3.2 million years ago and would offer valuable clues about the origins of humanity.

Lucy was named after the Beatles song "Lucy in the Sky with Diamonds".

The song was playing loudly all evening in the expedition camp after the hominid was discovered – and the name stuck.

The Power of Persuasion

The following catchy slogans capture the spirit of an era defined by iconic brands and creative advertising campaigns.

"I'd like to buy the world a coke"

Coca Cola

"Freewheelin' Ford"

Ford

"Campbell's in the cupboard is like money in the bank"

Campbell's Soup

"The times of your life"
Kodak

"Pepsi generation"
Pepsi

"You deserve a break today"
McDonald's

"Don't leave home without it"
American Express

"I'm stuck on Band-Aid"
Band-Aid

Supersonic Airmiles

On 21 January 1976, the first commercial Concorde planes took off simultaneously from London and Paris.

The groundbreaking flights, to Bahrain and Rio de Janeiro respectively, ushered in an era of supersonic travel for passengers, offering unprecedented speed and luxury.

"

The best thing that any business man can do with his few hours saved by flying supersonically is to have a few more Martinis.

"

New Scientist, 15 April 1971

Computer Revolution

In 1977, Steve Wozniak and Steve Jobs introduced one of the first successful home computers, the Apple II.

Offering features such as a built-in keyboard, colour graphics, a user-friendly design and a wide range of software applications, it played a crucial role in revolutionizing the personal computer industry.

"

You can use your Apple to analyze the stock market, manage your personal finances, control your home environment, and to invent an unlimited number of sound and action video games. That's just the beginning.

"

From an advert for the Apple II, 1979

Medical Miracle

The world's first test tube baby, Louise Brown, was born on 25 July 1978. She was conceived through in vitro fertilization (IVF), pioneered by British researchers Robert Edwards and Patrick Steptoe.

In 2010, Edwards won the Nobel Prize in Medicine for IVF, which has helped families conceive more than 5 million babies around the world.

"

I'll never get forget the day
I looked down the microscope
and saw something funny in
the cultures. I looked down the
microscope and what I saw was
a human blastocyst gazing up at
me. I thought: 'We've done it.'

"

Robert Edwards

Recalling the moment he first created a fertilized human
embryo in 1968, speaking in 2008

Tech Trailblazing

A remarkable surge in technological advancements paved the the way for transformative breakthroughs.
Here are five incredible innovations:

The release of the **microprocessor** by Intel in 1971 revolutionized the electronics industry.

The first **email** was sent in 1971, laying the groundwork for instant electronic messaging across vast distances.

Developed at Xerox PARC in California, **Ethernet** was a groundbreaking innovation in computer networking, which set the stage for the internet.

The first **magnetic resonance imaging (MRI)** exam on a live human patient was performed in July 1977.

Fiber optic technology, which uses thin strands of glass or plastic to transmit data using light signals, enabled faster and more reliable long-distance communication.

Happy Mistake

In 1977, Post-it notes were invented... by accident! Dr Spencer Silver, a scientist at 3M, was trying to create a strong adhesive but ended up developing a low-tack adhesive instead – which had the unique property of sticking lightly to surfaces and being easily removable.

Another 3M scientist recognized its potential and the ever-popular Post-it note was born.

66

There is really no way to
convey the remarkable sound
quality of this little machine.
You've got to hear it.

99

From an advert for the Sony Walkman, launched in 1979

66

This is a present from a small, distant world, a token of our sounds, our science, our images, our music, our thoughts and our feelings. We are attempting to survive our time so we may live into yours. We hope someday, having solved the problems we face, to join a community of galactic civilizations. This record represents our hope and our determination, and our good will in a vast and awesome universe.

99

Message carried on the *Voyager I* spacecraft, launched into space 5 September 1977